Developing Your Relationship With God

By

James and Linda Clark

authorHOUSE™

1663 LIBERTY DRIVE, SUITE 200
BLOOMINGTON, INDIANA 47403
(800) 839-8640
WWW.AUTHORHOUSE.COM

First published by AuthorHouse 11/01/05

ISBN: 1-4208-1636-5 (sc)
ISBN: 1-4208-1637-3 (dj)

Library of Congress Control Number: 2004099248

Printed in the United States of America
Bloomington, Indiana

This book is printed on acid-free paper.

TABLE OF CONTENTS

INTRODUCTION
CHAPTER ONE: DO YOU HAVE A RELATIONSHIP WITH GOD?

Over two thousand years ago on a Wednsday night, Jesus was captured, tortured, and crucified, for a crime in which he had no fault. He was buried on Thursday so that the prophesy in the word of God, might be fulfilled. Jesus loved us so much that he bled, suffered and died for us. There was no way I could know that Jesus loved me until he *showed* his love for me. The scripture tells us that God so loved the world that he gave his only begotten son, (the best that he had), to die for a sinful world. (St. John 3:16). John picked it up and said, "There is no greater love than this, that a man would lay down his life for a friend". (St. John 15:13). Jesus gave us a way out of sin, out of loneliness, out of misfortune, sorrow, poverty etc. He died so that we can over come these things and ourselves as well, so that we can love him. Who wouldn't want to develop a loving, lasting relationship with a magnificent man like this?

How is your relationship with God? Is it a close one? Most of us don't even know when God is talking to us. Do you know his voice? You have to live the life of God and obey him to even feel his presence. How can God have his way with you, and how can you have a relationship with him if you don't even know him? We don't have that thrill in God that we should have. You have to have a thrill (happiness) in God so that you can have church anywhere you go. You have to have something that will keep you when that feeling is gone. God wants to take you to another level in him. You need something within your spirit, after the music stops. You need something that, even when you don't have church, that thrill will not diminish. Consider your love. Do you love God? He declares in his word, "If you love me, you will keep my commandments.

We seem to have a constant relationship with one of three different people: God, the devil or ourselves. Having a relationship with self, and the devil, will only lead to sorrow and eternal damnation, but developing a relationship with God yields good health, prosperity, happiness and eternal life in glory. I have learned that the word of God can't get to rough for me because I know that the word is purposed to keep me on the right track, and to make me aware of areas in my life that need improvement. It then gives me the help I need to get those areas right. You should *want* God to come to your aide in those areas where help is needed.

God is still blessing us. That is enough excitement alone, to keep you encouraged. You know that God is still blessing when you begin to think about things that *could have* happened, but God didn't allow them to happen. We are living in a time where you have to be determined, and have your mind made up to go all the way with God. If your mind is not made up you will not be able to 'hang'. You *will* turn back. Your mind has to be made up to stay saved, and your motives have to be right. When you really love someone you will stick with them through thick and thin. Serving God is not all glamorous, it is work. You have to go into the vineyard and work. You have to be conditioned or you will give up. When Uncle Sam calls you into the army, he conditions you. He prepares you for everything you will possibly have to face. If your mind or motives are not conditioned when you are working in the vineyard for God, you will not stay in the vineyard. God conditions you when you have done what he has called you to do. After you have obeyed God, the devil will also show up. After you have finished preaching the gospel, the devil will show up to try you with every word of the Gospel that you have preached to others.

There are people that feel as if they can do anything, say anything, or have any kind of feeling, and still develop a sincere relationship with God. God has given us a plan for salvation (the bible) that we must follow. There are no exceptions and no short-cuts. You have to develop this relationship by yourself , in your home. When you develop this relationship with him, God will talk to you and reveal things unto you. If you allow God to talk to you at home, your leaders won't have to tell you about it when you go to church.

While developing your relationship with God, you must also witness to others and let them know the rewards and the benefits of having this joyous relationship with God. After you have witnessed to people and they decide to come to church with you, you have to break your self away from them so that they won't begin to see your shortcomings. This is why it is so important to let God fix and deliver every area in your life that has not come up to the requirements in his word. You have to allow the leaders of your church, to teach the people. It is your job to direct them to the man and woman of God. You may have a title, but you cannot 'pastor' the people in the church. It is your job to love the people, even if they are not like they are supposed to be in Christ. We have all sinned and come short of his glory. God does not want his people to be home, burdened down, or home or talking about each other. You do not have to carry the burdens of the people in the church. Whatever God told you to do you have to do it. Your spirit does not have to be bound because of what someone has said or what they have done. All you are required to do is what God has called you to do. We are trying to go higher in God, and it is not our job to find fault or criticize our brothers or sisters. We are in the same spiritual family, serving the same Lord.

Any time you hold things inside, you are hindering yourself. The worst thing you can do is try to perform a job without the anointing. You can't in any way, successfully carry out a job without God's anointing. The devil will do his best to get into every little thing to

4

stop you. He will use whatever tactic necessary, to prevent the Holy Ghost from moving and manifesting itself in you.

Your relationship with God should not be based on gifts and talents. These things come without repentance (anyone can have them). Your relationship with God, the Father, should be first priority in your life and it should be a powerful and fulfilling one. Your relationship with God should be greater than your relationship with your spouse, your children, your family, or your friends. God has to be first and everything else is secondary. Nothing and no one, can take the place of God. If you substitute anything else for him, don't expect it to prosper or come to any good.

You have to allow the things of God to engulf you in order to receive of him. I have learned that all of our blessings don't come from God. Did you know that those name brand shoes and the gold that you are wearing, didn't come from God? Some of those things we just went out and purchased ourselves. We plunged into that dept all by ourselves. God was in no way involved. That is why some people are in despair and are plagued with depression today. That is why the world is so laden with poverty. We depend on the pay we receive from our natural jobs. We feel as if the job is what is helping us to survive. Not so!! Do not get so wrapped up in a job that you cannot concentrate on God. In him is where your true blessing lie. When that job has folded, you are going to need God. Jobs are folding every day. Don't let anyone fool you. I don't care how good you are at your job, or how much of an asset you are to that job,

5

there is always someone that can do it better. Always keep God first, and he will bless you *through* your job. Concentrate on him.

When developing a relationship with God, we are not supposed to get mad or upset. Some say that they are working on rectifying this problem. This is one problem that we have to be swift in making right. If Jesus comes while we are still "working" on it, we are going to be left behind. What ever is wrong, be swift to rectify it. Don't let it just drag on and on. The word of God says not to let the sun go down on your wrath. Letting the problems and situations linger, allows the devil time to invade your mind and your spirit with negative things. If we are quick to rectify the problem, we demolish the plan of the enemy. If you go to bed with the problem, during your slumber (he won't let you rest), the enemy will have told you and shown you, so many things and will have made you feel so many different ways. Then you will have another problem to handle before you can even get to the true problem at hand. That is why God wants us to be swift in getting things right. The enemy knows when something is not the way it is supposed to be. He is excited because he knows that you have just given him ground to come in and do his thing.

Something that I have learned through the years, is that sometimes in a conflict, you can proceed to get your end of the matter rectified with a person, but they may not be willing to rectify their end. You may go to them and ask for forgiveness, but they may flat out refuse to accept your plea. The problem is then, no longer yours, because you have done your part. You have done what God has required of you. There will be broken fellowship between you and that person until they have followed the example you have set. You overcome evil with good. God has it all in control and he will work it out. Why are you worrying? All you need is a little faith, and trust in God to continue in him and to endure.

The church as a whole, has to get excited about working for God. If you cannot get excited in the church, the devil will persuade you to search elsewhere for excitement.

God has been good to us! When you walk into the sanctuary, you should be smiling because you know that you serve a God who can work out any situation and solve any problem. We serve a God who can do anything but fail.

You should strive to have an excellent relationship with God. When you have established a relationship with him, it will be obvious.

The magnitude of your relationship with God is based on your relationship with his people. Because your relationship with God is based on your relationship with people, you have to be able to adjust yourself to deal with every type of person. God does not just direct you to people that you like, but he directs you to all types of people. You can not be affective in church if you are holding something within you against other people.

The word of God says in I John 4:4, greater is he that is in you than he that is in the world. If the greater one resides in you, than you should have no problem with other people. Sometimes there is something within you that is not right and that blemish in your vessel is made apparent by the way you deal with other people. You have

7

to be totally delivered from yourself (flesh) and from your feelings. When you have a problem with your feelings you will not be able to get along with anyone. If you do not forgive people, you will cause a break in your relationship with God.

You have to be able to master (control) your feelings. Your feelings will dictate to you that you are not happy, but sad, and that everything is not okay, but something is wrong. Your own feelings keep you from dealing with one another. In order to get the job done that God wants you to do you have to release your feelings so that you will be able to reach your brothers and sisters. Feelings can easily dominate you. When God comes into your life he transforms you into a different creature. Your walk, talk, attitude, and character are new and Christ-like. You have to allow God to save you enough so that you will be able to put your old self back into place if , and when it tries to show up again (it will try to show up).

The scripture says, Oh wretched man, who shall deliver you. Although Paul had performed great things he was still not pleasing and acceptable to God. You can do great work for God and still be in a shell. You have to be made new to do what God has called you to do. If you allow yourself to stay in that old mode, you will not get with the vision of your church ministry. As long as you stay in that shell, you will not be able to see people in the appropriate image. You will see all the negative qualities and never the good, in people.

It is important to operate in unity. Where there is unity, there is strength and pleasantness. In other words, there is a good feeling present. As long as you draw back, you will not be able to move in God. If you do not get wounded or hurt in the church, you will not be all that God has called you to be. These wounds and hurts are destined to make you better. You have to be able to take something. How will you know whether or not you can take anything if you are never confronted with problems or situations?

Just to reiterate; in order to develop a relationship with God, you must first develop a relationship with people. Be mindful that it is not your duty to get to know the person for yourself (there personal business) but to get to know the inner man. When you began to go outside of the realm of God while trying to get to know people, you will begin to nose into their business. Your main focus should be what the individual has in his heart to do for the Lord and not what happened yesterday between them and their spouse. .

Developing a relationship with God is not always easy. People will continue to come to church when everything is alright, but on this journey to developing a relationship with God, everything is not always going to be alright. It is a daily thing. Sometimes you have to evaluate your relationship with people. For example, you may say, "I do not like the way my relationship is with sister Johnson or Evangelist Jones, because we are not talking about the right things when we get together". You have to develop your relationship with God and with people the right way, or you will find yourself out of the realm of God. We often give excuses as to why we don't attend church. You cannot afford to give up for anything. The word of God say to neglect not to assemble yourselves together. You can not give up on God for your spouse, your children or any one else. Some say that they don't attend church because someone in the church has done something to hurt them, but that is also just an excuse not to attend church. No one can really hurt you unless you allow them. People on your job hurt you, your spouse may hurt you, but you continue to go back. Why won't you continue to go back to church, where you can get supernatural help and healing?

When you get in church, receive your healing, your blessing, your deliverance, your rebuke and your chastisement. It is all for your good. Many people try to pretend that the particular word preached, was not for them. We like to throw the message off on other people when we know beyond a shadow of a doubt, that God was talking directly to us.

We need faith to get healing within our spirit. Sometimes evil spirits and habits, attach themselves to you. These spirits 'tag along' because things that you are doing, you are doing in the flesh. All you have to do to alleviate this problem is to begin doing work for God, doing those things that are in accordance to his word, and you will lose those 'tag along' spirits. You have to build up your faith until you can hear from God. You want to be able to hear from God in your home, on your job or anywhere he would see fit to talk to you.

Remember that no one can offend you unless you allow yourself to be offended. When you realize who you are, and remember that it is not that person but the devil speaking through that person, you will not get offended. If you allow your flesh to rise up, you will retaliate and you will be no better that they are. The devil will have used you as well. If you allow flesh, it will dictate to you how to respond, but you don't have to listen. There are some things that you cannot handle yourself. In these situations you need to pray and ask God to help you and to help the other person as well.

CHAPTER TWO: POSSESSING GOD''S SPIRIT

TRUE REPENTANCE

To begin a relationship with God, we must repent of all of our sins. The church world has to be aware of what Godly repentance really is. A Godly repentance is a sincere repentance after which you will not do that wrong, anymore. There is to much reoccurrence of the same things, therefore, true repentance have not yet occurred. We as people of God have to make a permanent change. There is no turning back. We do not have time to repent and then repeat the things we did yesterday. God is calling for true repentance from the pulpit to the back door; from the Bishop to every one else in the building. When a child of God repents, he is forgiven and restored and what he has done is rectified. You should not allow problems or situations to linger or last for months. In order to have a true relationship with God, true repentance must take place. When true repentance occurs that very thing that you repented of should serve as a thorn in your flesh. It should constantly remind you of the situation you were in and the consequences suffered from that situation, so that you will be determined not to do that, say that, or allow that to happen again.

The bible says to forgive your brother 70 times seven, times a day. There is not even that many hours in a day. You are not even around them that many times a day. We are supposed to forgive them that many times a day and we carry one thing around within us for days and weeks at a time. If you are praying, you have to free your vessel of this hindrance. If you are praying for anything to be changed in your life, you have to learn to forgive and get all the negative things out of your vessel.

THE SPIRIT OF GOD

The spirit of Christ works on the inside, but it only works according to you. If you do not fast, read, or pray, the spirit will not work for you. We are trying to build and establish a relationship with God. In order to build this relationship, the foundation has to be properly laid. Once you get saved there must be a change in you. Your attitude and your character must change. We often get confused because we feel like God is blessing us in spite of what we are doing wrong. The blessings of God comes with requirements. God will bless you to go to hell if you do not live right. Once you get saved, the spirit of God takes control of your vessel. We are supposed to be changing everyday through the spirit of God. The people that you use to know should not recognize your character now. They should not recognize you as that person they used to drink with, and party with. Everything about you should be different. Someone should be able to say that you are not carrying yourself like you generally do, or act like they have known you to act. Jesus is coming back for a church without spot or wrinkle. He is not coming back for a church that is *trying* to get it together.

We have repented and now we are moving on to higher hights and deeper depths in God. Every one that says they are saved, are not. A saved person does not lie, cheat, steal or have a spirit of jealousy against another person. The spirit of jealousy comes from the adversary. When you acquire a spirit of jealousy, it broadens the way for other demonic spirits to occupy your vessel.

Once you are truly saved you have to have a victorious spirit regardless of the situation. You should never be weak when the God you serve has all power in his hands. You have to resist the devil and obey God in order to be strong. Once you fall in love with the things of God, and with his will, you will become strong. As you maintain your salvation, you will eventually face yourself (flesh). Don't try and put everything on the devil. Flesh is the initiator of most of our problems. All you have to do is to check out how you feel, how you are talking, and what you are thinking, to let yourself know whether or not you are operating in the spirit of God, or in your own flesh.

When you are truly happy, any one should be able to get along with you. Obedience has a lot to do with your salvation. You are saved and you grow, because you have changed and you do those

14

commandments written in the word of God. Obedience to God is of vital importance to your salvation.

II Corinthians 5:17
Therefore if any man be in Christ, he is a new creature: old things are passed away; behold, all things are become new.

The problem we face within this verse of scripture is that one minute we are in the spirit of Christ and the next minute we have reverted to the old man. When you become a new creature your old way, old habits, that old personality and your old attitude will become new.

Are you performing spiritual things? Fussing, arguing, complaining, and doubting, is not spiritual. If any man be saved, the blood of Jesus has washed you and the spirit of God dwells within you. If you find yourself doing old deeds, you have assured yourself that you are not yet that new creature that God intended you to be. When you possess the spirit of God, it will seek to do the things of God. We ourselves often seek after the wrong things and get over-excited about them. When you become new your mind, and your entire being changes, as well as your will and your desire to please God. If reading God's word don't excite you then something is wrong with your salvation.

You are new when the things you have been desiring for your flesh, is no longer of importance. When you become new you seek after spiritual gifts. The spirit of God is so good that it will let you know *before* you start preaching to the church, that you need to first be a good husband or a good wife at home. The spirit of God will not have you put to shame. We should strive to have our very lives, wrapped up in the things of God.

How much time do you spend in the presence of God? You have to be in his presence to develop a relationship with him. Our love for God is lacking because we do not stay in his presence long enough. We tend to spend more time on worldly pleasures and things that satisfy the flesh, than we do on things that would edify and benefit the spirit.

If you are a new creature you need to check to see if that rage or that temper that you used to have, is released from your vessel. You have to rid yourself of all filthiness so that you can become a true witness for God. You cannot be a true witness for God when you and your spouse are spiritually separated. The very way you act in your home, will be the exact way you will present yourself in church. If you are not loving right at home, you will not love the people in church. If you are fussing and arguing at home, it won't take much for you to argue and fuss in the church.

You have to take inventory of yourself to make sure that those old habits have diminished. To find out whether they are truly gone, when something happens, watch and see whether the old habits resurface. Jesus will go down into the valley deep to bring you out of any problem or situation and deliver you from any habit or evil spirit. When he brings you out, don't ever allow yourself be found in the valley anymore. Is there a habit that you used to have that has a tendency to resurface every now and then? You have to fast, pray, and read the word of God, and let him deliver you. Constantly check yourself to keep yourself free of those old habits.

Any time something is continually on your mind, that is something that is still inside of you. It is a blemish in your vessel. If it continues to stay on your mind, it will eventually take effect. It will cease to be just a thought and will become an action. You have to replace those negative things in your mind, with the word of God. Read, fast, pray and do the works of God and you will be delivered from all of your habits.

There are some things that we do and habits that we have, that *we* have to make go away. These are things that we love to do even though we *know* that it is wrong to do them. *You* have to be *determined* not to do those things anymore. You have to make the choice and decide whether those habits are worth your soul salvation. NO they are not!!

Our relationship with God is false at times and it is not pleasing to him. Your relationship with God should be true. Before I finish you will find out why the power of God is diminished in your life. Although the power is available, it is diminished.

I Corinthians 6:19
What? Know ye not that your body is the temple of the Holy Ghost which is in you, which ye have of God, and ye are not your own?

The Holy Ghost should rest, rule, and abide in your temple. If you are not living right, there will be few signs of manifestation of the Holy Ghost. God never takes the Holy Ghost away from you but it does not operate when you are engaged in wrong. On the day of judgement God will take his spirit back. The Holy Ghost is God's spirit. When his spirit resides on the inside of you, everything else (fleshly ways) is supposed to be banished from you. When the holy ghost is not operating within you, you will be weak. You will be mighty one day and weak the next day. When you have the spirit of God you are no longer your own and you can't do what you want to do: flesh can no longer dictate to you. You know that you have not lived according to God's word, yet you continue to come to church and praise God. You are not available for God to use all day, but when you come to church it's Hallelujah, Thank You Jesus. God won't use you like this.

1 Corinthians 6:20
For ye are bought: therefore glorify God in your body, and in your spirit, which are God's.

Once you get save you are bought with a price. You are supposed to do what God tells you to do. Be obedient to his word. You glorify God in your body when you let God have control of your body. When you glorify God in your body, he is pleased with you. Sometimes you can do good deeds and still not be in the spirit. Good things come from your body when your spirit is controlled by God. Remember that no good things come from the flesh. Most of the time your spirit is focused on natural things, such as your children, spouse, bills, etc. When God has control of your spirit it is concerned about what God wants it to do. The spirit is in control when you do what God tells you to do.

11Corinthians 5:10
For we must all appear before the judgement seat of Christ; that every one may receive the things done in his body, according to that he hath done, whether it be good or bad.

We have to stand before the judgement seat of Christ and give an account for everything we say, feel think, and do. You have to receive a reward for everything you have done, both the good and the bad. Everything that this body does that is not of Christ, you have to give an account for. You will have to appear before God for being a hypocrite. Some people are holy while they are in church and when they get with their family they act just like their family acts.

11 Corinthians 5:11
Knowing therefore the terror of the Lord, we persuade men; but we are made manifest unto God; and I trust also are made manifest in your consciences.

We have to know the terror, wrath, and vengeance of God. If we really knew the terror of God we would make haste to straighten up. God is an awesome God. God can kill and individual and medical science will call it a heart attack because they can find no other logical explanation. Once we really learn the terror of God and what he does to liars, cheaters, whore-mongers, backbiters, hypocrites, people that pretend to love him, etc., we will stop our mess. God is going to give them their portion in the lake of fire. Even when you are in a room, behind close doors, God knows exactly what you are doing. He sits high and looks low. There are husbands and wives at war with each other in the home, and they come to church pretending to be so in love. All of this will be presented on the day of Judgement. It is Hallelujah when you get to church but what was it before you got there? When you dance and know that your spirit is not right, all you are doing is wearing out the soles of your shoes and spreading that bad spirit around. It is very important to get yourself right. You never know what type of influence you are having on the people around you. It is time for all of us to be real and become more alert to flesh, the adversary and their tactics.

Ecclesiastes 12:13

Let us hear the conclusion of the whole matter: Fear God, and keep his commandments: for this is the whole duty of man.

We have to hear the whole conclusion of the matter. Do you really fear God? If you really feared God, you would stop sinning.

We do not fear God because we do anything we feel we are big enough to do. God may have told you to stop what you are doing, fifteen years ago, but you are still doing the very same thing. You will not fear God unless you reverence him. We come into church any kind of way. Some of us are all messed up and we think that God's commandments say do what we want to do. When you read the bible and do not obey it you are not keeping God's commandments. You have to obey God's commandments everyday, not just when you feel like it. We can not lay the commandments of God down. When you can lay them down whenever you want to, you never reverenced them from the start.. Keeping God's commandments keeps us in right fellowship with him. When you keep his commandments you do exactly what he says to do. You can't do one part and neglect another.

When you develop a relationship with God, he will give you a plan for your life. When you use God's plan you will not lack in anything, because his plan has everything that you need.

Ecclesiastes 12:14
For God shall bring every work into judgement, with every secret thing, whether it be good, or whether it be evil.

God will bring every work and everything that we have ever done into judgment. Most of our works are not good. Although *we* may have forgotten them, God will surely bring them all into judgment. God has it on record when you laid up with Joe and when you slept with Sally. He has it written down when you lied to that brother and when you stole from sister. He also has it on record when you stole from him (When you didn't pay your tithes and offerings-OUCH!). God will bring into judgement, everything that you have ever done, and everything that you were supposed to do for him but didn't do.

Let the anointing of God take over in your life. When the anointing takes over it endows you with power from God. You have to constantly work on your inward power because that is the power that will connect with God when he returns. When he returns, you will be caught up to meet him in the air.

When you allow yourself to be entangled with something that is not of God, your anointing will not operate as it should. You may not even feel the anointing. When you allow something other than God to dominate your spirit, it will leave you with a bad feeling. You can see someone else telling lies or doing something wrong and it will affect you. Let me illustrate using a married couple. If either person in the marriage has a problem, they will confide in their spouse. If that spouse that is hearing the problem isn't careful, they will agree with the other, instead of helping them because they love their spouse. We have to help each other but we have to do it in the right way. Suppose your wife came home crying and claiming that the people at her church, hurt her in some way; before you try and find out what part she played in the uproar or if there really was a problem to begin with, you would probably become angry with the people at the church and tell her to never to go there again. It is hard to see the faults of a person that you really love or who is very close to you.

You have to be very careful with disagreements because they stir up anger and negative emotion. The devil will bring opposition between you and someone else to keep discord amongst the people of God. Most of the time people are not saved enough to say or bold enough to say that they don't agree with some one or something. People's feelings and thoughts seem to be of greater importance to them. They care more about developing a relationship with people rather than with God. You have to be saved enough to take opposition. When you cannot take opposition, flesh is in operations. You have to release the things of the flesh so that you can be real for God. You have to get to the point where you can have a disagreement and still possess your love. You have to remember to keep your eyes on the prize of eternal life and let nothing or no one deter you.

Psalms 85:9
Surely his salvation is nigh them that fear him; that glory may dwell in our land.

Salvation is near the people that fear the Lord. Even in their mouth. There are always opportunities to get saved. How many times have God spoken to you and you left the church and did the same things again? Yet you say that you are saved. When you get genuinely saved, you will stop living in the flesh, but live in the spirit of God. If you are not saved at home or on your job, then you will not be saved at church. There is supposed to be glory living in, and around you, *if* you are living for God. We try to get so many things without God. It wont last and it won't be productive.

Psalms 85:10
Mercy and truth are met together; righteousness and peace have kissed each other.

We need mercy and truth, not confusion, poverty and hard times. Mercy and truth are supposed to join, when it comes to the characteristics of Christ. We neglect to obey God but we are always wanting him to do something for us, give us something or get us out of some situation. Righteousness and peace are supposed to surround us everywhere we go. You have to show the love of God to all people.

Psalms 85:11-13
11. Truth shall spring out of the earth; and righteousness shall look down from heaven.
12. Yea, the Lord shall give that which is good; and our land shall yield her increase.
13. Righteousness shall go before him; and shall set us in the way of his steps.

This will happen if we do the will of God. The Lord will give us that which is good, including land. When you hear God he prepares the way for you. When you do not hear him, you have to prepare your own way. Your way does not produce *lasting* prosperity.

Proverbs 8:32
Now therefore hearken unto me, O ye children: for blessed are they that keep my ways.

Hearken means to listen or attend to. God is saying to give him your ear. Those who hear, remember, and apply what the word says, will be blessed.

Meditate on God and keep your mind in perfect peace.

Revelations 3:20
Behold, I stand at the door, and knock: if any man hear my voice, and open the door, I will come in to him, and will sup with him, and he with me.

Jesus is standing at the door knocking. If he has to knock at the door, the door must have been closed. You have to hear God knocking before you can open the door. He is knocking so that he can cleanse us of everything that is wrong within us. When you open your heart unto him, you are allowing him to do this. Remember that you have to die for yourself, and die in yourself so that you can live for the Lord.

CHAPTER THREE:
FAITH IN YOUR RELATIONSHIP

Some people feel that they can do plenty without developing a relationship with God. Your relationship with God must be one of faith. You have to expect God to do all that he has promised to us in his word. Faith controls the things that we do not have but really need.

FAITH IN ACTION

Hebrews 11:1
Now faith is the substance of things hoped for, the evidence of things not seen.

Faith pertains to the things that we are not anticipating. You cannot see it or possess it with your physical eyes, but you can visualize it with spiritual sight. In some instances, you can hope for things for so long that you lose faith. Don't allow other things to shake your faith. Your faith is beneficial to your spirit. When you lose faith, your personality is affected. We allow so many things to substitute or take away our faith. You have to remember that without faith, it is impossible to please God, and our goal in life should be to please him and do all that he has required of us to do.

Romans 1:17

For therein is the righteousness of God revealed from faith to faith: as it is written, The Just Shall Live By Faith.

We are justified by faith. There are things that we cannot obtain unless there is an increase of our faith. Faith keeps us. God honors faith. The word of God lets us know that faith comes by hearing and hearing by the word of God. (Romans 10:17). Most of what we hear today is not faith, because it does not build or edify your spirit. Your faith will not be increased unless you believe and receive the word of God. You have to hear the right things to build the inner man (spirit). Most people only hear the word when they come to church, but unless you are building on the inner man, you will die spiritually. The spirit needs the nourishment of the word of God to flourish and to grow. The way you live is the very thing that affects your faith. You have to live in accordance to the word and the spirit of God.

We really do not know how to believe God for what we want. His word says that if you live right, you can ask for anything. When you know that you are not living right, you will hesitate to ask God for what you need. If you live the way God tells you, there will not be a shortage of anything in your life. He will supply all of your needs. You can not base your salvation on a song, a sermon, or emotions. You have to base it on faith and the development of a relationship with God.

There are things that are freely given that we still won't be able to claim, because of our lack of faith. Everything that God has for you is freely given but it is dependant upon your faith. You cannot be unbalanced in God. God does not want you looking blessed naturally while the spiritual man goes neglected. The word of God tells us to seek first the Kingdom of God (Matthew 6:33). We love nice things but our spirits are not always right to receive them. You have to be saved the way God intended, and then these nice things that you desire, will be added unto you.

Romans 10:17

So then faith cometh by hearing, and hearing by the word of God.

This verse of scripture has to be applied to your life in order for your faith to increase. You have to hear the word of God. Although there are many that hear but don't believe, there are many that believe because they have heard. To even begin to have faith, you have to first hear. When your faith does not increase your relationship with God does not progress. You have to hear from the word of God. Even when you are working on a natural job, you have to take time to meditate on the word of God. You really don't know what God wants until you develop a relationship with him. Reading the word of God and receiving it are two different things, for the letter killeth but it is the spirit that giveth life (II Corinthians 3:6).

Faith comes by hearing therefore we have to hear when the word of God is being given. You cannot surround yourself with things that do not produce faith. As you hear the right things, your faith will become stronger. Your relationship with God should not be based on gifts and talents.

When you refuse to hear the word of God you are refusing to hear the very thing you need to increase your faith. You are refusing your blessings. When you have no faith you can not receive your healing or deliverance. When your faith is not building, you will not have a zeal for God. You will be satisfied doing what you are doing.

If your flesh does not die every time you get offended, it will hinder you spiritually. When you allow yourself to feel everything it causes you to waver in the spirit. Unless you build on your faith, you will not be able to take anything. If your faith is not built up, the slightest incidence will cause you to leave the church. When you let things bother you it alarms the devil to where your weaknesses are.

God will not fail you or let you down. That is why you have to put all your faith in him, and not in man. When you put your faith in a man or a woman, you will find out that, when you don't do like they want you to do, they will leave you. God will never leave you nor forsake you (Hebrews 13:5). You have to get to the point that your relationship is between you and God. Don't let man interfere. When you get into trouble, God is the one that comes to your rescue. You have to allow your faith to rise up and be determined that your trust and relationship is with God.

1Timothy 6:11
But thou, O man of God, flee these things; and follow after righteousness, godliness, faith, love, patience, meekness.

We are supposed to conduct ourselves as children of God. If it is not righteousness it is not of God. Godliness is the character that we should be pursuing. God does not accept anything less. We have to have patience (perseverance, endurance) with each other. Even when people cut you short you have to continue to have patience with them. It is bad when you can have patience with sinners but can not have it with your brothers and sisters in Christ. We must have the love of God and the same meekness (gentleness) that he has.

1Timothy 6:12
Fight the good fight of faith, lay hold on eternal life, where-unto thou art also called, and hast professed a good profession before many witnesses.

We must fight the good fight of faith to make it to heaven. Your desire should be to have a sweet and humble faith walk in God. You should have a strong, and quickened desire to want to develop a relationship with him. You have to strive to do good and not hold things within your spirit. If someone hurts you, you should get it right before you proceed or attempt to do anything else. When you approach someone they are not supposed to put up a shield against you. Only when you fight the good fight of faith will you be able to lay hold on eternal life. This is a good fight and it will yield a bountiful harvest. You have declared that you are save and you have to be determined that you are not going to lose you faith behind anyone or anything. Be very afraid to lose your faith, knowing that without it, you can in no way, lay hold on eternal life with Christ in glory.

11 Timothy 4:7
I have fought a good fight, I have finished my course, I have kept the faith.

You have to realize that you will not live forever and you have to do things God's way. Our lives are a course and we have to accomplish what God wants us to do before that course (life) is finished. Our resume should reflect what we have done, and that we have done things the right way. Faith and works coincide. You can not play and mess around with people otherwise you will not keep the faith. God has everything that you need. He will put you through a test. If God does not trust you he will not give you anything to do.

James2:17-26

17. Even so faith, if it hath not works, is dead, being alone.

18. Yea, a man my say, Thou hast faith, and I have works: show me thy faith without thy works, and I will show thee my faith by my works.

19. Thou believest that there is one God; thou doest well: the devils also believe, and tremble.

20. But wilt thou know, O vain man, that faith without works is dead?

21. Was not Abraham our father justified by works, when he had offered Isaac his son upon the alter?

22. Seest thou how faith wrought with his works, and by works was faith made perfect?

23. And the scriptures was fulfilled which saith, ABRAHAM BELIEVED GOD, AND IT WAS IMPUTED UNTO HIM FOR RIGHTEOUSNESS: and he was called the friend of God.

24. Ye see then how that by works a man is justified, and not by faith only.

25. Likewise also was not Rahab the harlot justified by works, when she had received the messengers, and had sent them out another way?

26. For as the body without the spirit is dead, so faith without works is dead also.

Faith has to have works along with it. Just professing it with your mouth will not save you. You can not tell me that you have faith if you do not have works. You cannot make me believe that you have faith if I never see any fruit from it. James says here, to show him your faith without your works and he will let his works speak for his faith. If you are content with just saying you have faith and do nothing to prove that you really believe God, then you are doing no more than unbelivers do. They also believe.

You have to have great faith. Abraham had to offer his only son for sacrifice. He had a working faith that believed God would provide. We don't have many Abraham's in today's church. Abraham's faith was made perfect because of his works. He was justified by his works; not just his faith alone. Most of us would have lost out or given up on our salvation. You cannot believe in God without obeying him. Let your faith be productive of good works. Acting on your faith will make it grow to be perfect, and thus make us friends of God. You have to do something. You can not say that you are a missionary and you are not doing anything that signifies a missionary. When you do that you are a liar and a hypocrite too. You have to carry out a particular work. You're work sets you apart from other people. People who work in the church are the most valuable people.

Rahab did a little faith work. She was a bad woman but she did a little work. She received the messengers even though it could have been hazardous to her own life. You have to have some works or your faith is dead. Visualize faith as your root, and know that if it produces no fruit, it is dead. Good works is the fruit of faith and we must possess both. One without the other will not justify us.

11 Thessalonians 1:3

We are bound always to thank God for you, brethren, as it is meet, because that your faith groweth exceedingly, and the charity of every one of you all toward each other aboundeth;

You are bound to your brothers and sisters regardless of what they do or say. Faith works by love. Where it grows, love will abound. You have to hurry up and get some faith so that your faith for everyone would abound. When you say you are through with people, or that you just give up on them, you are out of the will of God. Your faith has to build up until you are able to get along with other people. Faith must be exercised, tried, and kept. Do you think your faith will not be tried on your job? God never said how or where your faith was going to be tried. If you believe on him, God will work it out. In order to have an increase in your faith you have to shut your mouth and allow God to try your faith, exercise your faith, and keep you, what ever way he wants to. Do not think that it is strange when people say they are saved and continue to slap you spiritually. You have to be made by those people. You have to hold on to faith while people are talking about you, and remember that they are helping you to get somewhere in Christ. You have to be able to take it, and not become carnal minded. You have to endure these things by faith, and with patience, knowing that God will intervene and make everything alright.

Hebrews 10:35

Cast not away therefore your confidence, which hath great recompense of reward.

Don't let anyone rob you of your confidence in God. Hold on to it, for it will bring great reward if you do. The devil will use people to rob you of this confidence. As soon as you change spiritual uniforms, you faith has stopped. When you allow yourself to change uniforms, you have to go back to where you started and begin again. Every time you fall in an area of your life, it leaves a lasting effect on you. It shows that you can be hurt again in that area. If anyone hits that particular area you are ready to fuss and get mad. You can never overcome people until you get along with them. You can not preach, teach, or sing to anyone until you overcome them. You are going to be tempted in so many ways. You have to count it all joy because it is making and molding you into what God wants you to be. When you count it all joy, you can not get malice and hatred in your heart. When people talk about you or when they hang your name up on a sign post, count it all joy. When you know that you are innocent you can count it all joy. When you know that you have given it all that you have, count it all joy.

James 1:1-7

1. James, a servant of God and of the Lord Jesus Christ, to the twelve tribes which are scattered abroad, greeting.

35

2. My brethren, count it all joy when ye fall into divers temptations;

3. Knowing this, that the trying of your faith worketh patience.

4. But let patience have her perfect work, that ye may be perfect and entire, wanting nothing.

5. If any of you lack wisdom, let him ask of God, that giveth to all men liberally, and upbraideth not; and it shall be given him.

6. But let him ask in faith, nothing wavering. For he that wavereth is like a wave of the sea driven with the wind and tossed.

7. For let not that man think that he shall receive anything of the Lord.

The trying of your faith produces patience. Your faith has to be tried. In the midst of your trials, you must keep your joy. If you can not take anything then you have no faith. You cannot fall into a sad state, or you will faint in the midst of your trials. We have to let patience have her perfect work. When we deal with (bare) our trials and persecutions, and do it with joy, then we have surely allowed patience to have her perfect work. God is then pleased. While your faith is being tested, give God the praise. We do not have much patience when we hear things that we do not like. You have to be perfect in your love with people. You have to arrive at the point that no matter what happens it does not bother you because God already knows. I want my faith to withstand and not be shaken. You do not want to have any trouble when Jesus comes back. I do not want

Jesus to come back while I have ill feelings toward people. The word of God is your lifeline.

It is not faith when you desire what someone else have. When you are wavering in the spirit you do not have faith. If you want something today, and tomorrow you have a change of heart, you are wavering. Whatever you have made up your mind to do, pursue it. Our faith tends to waver as soon as something goes wrong. One day you are on the mountain top and the next day you are in the valley. Your spirit is back and forth, in and out of the presence of God. One minute you are for an individual and the next minute you are against them. One minute you are going all the way with God and the next minute you just don't know who you are serving. When your faith is not built up, self (flesh) will show up, and no one will be able to get along with you. No one can get along with the old man because it is mean, stubborn, etc. You can not get anything from God when you are wavering.

1Peter 5:7
Casting all your care upon him; for he careth for you.

Trust in God with your whole heart, mind, body, and spirit. No matter what the hardship, he said we can cast them all on him because he cares. God will release you of these cares. Do you ever wonder who will try your faith. Sometimes *you* do things that cause people to try your faith. Remember that your faith is much more precious than gold.

Matthew 9:29

Then touched he their eyes, saying, According to your faith be it unto you.

Christ healed the blind men according to their faith. Their cure was based on the level of their faith. Pertaining to faith, you have to allow the word of God to build upon *your* faith by your obedience to the word. When you do not obey the word, your faith will deteriorate. You healing is based on your faith. You can not allow other people to side track you or to question your faith. As long as you know that God is pleased with your faith, it doesn't matter what other people may think or say. Your faith does not only apply to healing but to everything that concerns Jesus. If you have no faith don't expect anything to happen.

Mark 9:17-22

17. And one of the multitude answered and said, Master, I have brought unto thee, my son, which hath a dumb spirit;

18. And wheresoever he taketh him, he tareth him: and he foameth , and gnasheth with his teth, and pineth away: and I spake to thy disciples that they should cast him out; and they could not.

19. He answereth him, and saith, O thou faithless generation, how long shall I be with you? How long shall I suffer you? Bring him unto me.

20. And they brought him unto him: and when he saw him, straightway the spirit tare him; and he fell on the ground, and wallowed, foaming.
21. And he asked his father, how long since this came unto him? And he said, Of a child.
22. And ofttimes it hath cast him into the fire, and into the waters, to destroy him: but if thou canst do anything, have compassion on us, and help us.

Jesus' disciples did not have enough faith, and thus could not give this chid possessed with a dumb spirit, any sort of relief. Jesus had come to his aid just in time. Jesus asked how long must he be among his faithless disciples. How long will Jesus have to tell us the same things over and over again?

The scripture speaks about foaming at the mouth and wallowing. Sometimes that is what it takes to get the devil out of you. If you are not right you do not need to be working around the alter. You are a false witness when you are laying hands on people and you are not right yourself. When you are not operating in the spirit of God, you need to sit down. The spirit of God is humble, gentle and sweet.

How long have you been the way you are? Things that are hindering your relationship with God are the things that you have to get rid of. We sometimes bring childhood problems and situations into our relationship with God. We cannot do this.

We have to maintain a maturity level in Christ. If you are not mature at all times, you will be continually hurt and offended. You cannot be mature only when you are in the presence of the man or woman of God. You have to be mature when you have to relate to other people as well If we can just believe in the power of God; hardened hearts will be softened, spiritual sicknesses will be cured, and we can hold out til the end.

The woman with the issue of blood is a prime example of faith in action.

Matthew 9:20-22

20. And behold, a woman, which was diseased with an issue of blood twelve years, came behind him, and touched the hem of his garment:

21. For she said within herself. If I may but touch his garment, I shall be whole.

22. But Jesus turned him about, and when he saw her, he said, Daughter, be of good comfort; thy faith hath made thee whole. And the woman was made whole from that hour.

This woman had a poison in the blood. She had a familiar affliction (one that people generally didn't have). She had something rare. Sometimes we can have a problem and it seems like no one else in the world has that problem but you. There is always someone else who has already walked in your shoes. Every pair of shoes that were made, someone has tried them on before they were put in the box.

There are a lot of sicknesses in the world today. Before we will love, we will hate. Before we would do better, we would be worse. Before we would encourage, we would tare down. Before we appreciate, we would find a way to talk negative.

This woman (Veronica), was different than most of us. She was dealing with a few things. She was sick with this disease and to add to her aggravation, she was impoverished because she had spent all of her money on the best doctors and they still had done her no good. We would have lost our love, our joy, our conversation would change from positive to negative, we would dry up in the church, and we would just totally change. Veronica made up in her mind that she was going to get her healing. Her faith was in action. You don't have to get mean and cold when you find yourself in a mess. If you walk and talk right, God has to deliver. He won't show up if you are not in his will. Get in his will and stay right there. Burdened down and rejected, but stay right there and watch him show up on your behalf.

Imagine in your mind being sick with disease for twelve years. Twelve years is a long time to deal with anything. Check out your situation. You have to be like Veronica. She had built up her trust. Whatever you are going through, stand up! Take it like a woman/man. Don't take it lying down.

In twelve years Veronica could probably analyze the road her condition had taken her. She spent all of her money and went to the best physicians, only to find that they couldn't do her any good. That is enough for most people today to lose all hope and throw in the towel. Refuse to quit. Situation after situation may present themselves, but make up in your mind that you will not quit.

Veronica had made up in her mind that she was going to get her healing, because she had heard of the fame of Jesus. She had great faith in him and in his power. She heard that he was healing the sick, raising the dead, and feeding the hungry. She made up in her mind that this man could heal her and she was going to get her healing. She had to press her way through the crowd. You have to press your way through difficult times to get where you need to be. After she had made up her mind, she wouldn't take no for an answer. Keep on in the will of God no matter what people say. That is what hinders a lot of people today. Everyone has an interpretation of your problem. They haven't walked the mile that you have walked, but they try to know what you are dealing with.

Veronica had a hard time getting to Jesus. She had to travel for miles to reach him. There was a lot of people around Jesus that didn't want anything. Most people today would have given up at the sight of the multitude, but not Veronica. Most of us are too secret and too proud to get help from God. If someone can help me, I don't care if they know what my problem or situation is. There were so many in the multitude when she got there but she pressed on, because she wanted something from Jesus. Veronica believed that if she could just touch the hem of his garment she knew that she would be made whole. She believed that he had such an overflowing of healing virtue, that all she had to do was to touch his garment: not the person, but just his garment, and she would be cured of her sickness. Her faith was rising. Even today you have to believe God and press your way. Even with no money or the fact that you don't

42

know how you are going to get out of your situation, you have to press your way anyhow. The people around Veronica didn't pay her any mind, but her focus was on Jesus.. If you keep your eyes on Jesus, the problem or situation won't bother you anymore. You have that faith in God to take it to him and leave it there. You are going to the highest source. You have witnessed what man can do and found that it was not enough. Veronica was full of this issue, but she pushed her way through the crowd. No matter what shape you are in, you have to get to Jesus. There are times that you may feel rejected, put down, broke, etc., but don't quit. God has a way to bless you anyhow. When Veronica got to Jesus, the disciples were guarding him so that the crowd wouldn't press in on him. Sometimes people will hold you back and keep you from getting to God. Veronica's faith stood up. She had to reach through the disciples to touch Jesus. She wasn't standing at this time. The crowd had beaten her down to her knees. This is just how fierce the crowd was. All she needed was his hem, to be made whole. Whether you have to walk, crawl, or run, do what you have to do to get to Jesus. He is your help. Whatever it takes to get your miracle, you do just that. Veronica had the faith in Christ that we need today. Her physical cure was the works of her faith. Remember that God is a good God and he wants to see us healthy, happy and prosperous.

CHAPTER FOUR: DEVELOPING A PRAYER LIFE IN GOD

Prayer is another area that is very important in developing a relationship with God.

We all need a praying spirit. When we pray, we must remember to pray for others, particularly for our enemies and those who have done us wrong. If we have done wrong to others, before we pray, we must go and be reconciled to them. This is the way we can get forgiveness for our sins.

When we are working we still need to be praying. We are living in a praying time. If we could pray as much as we worry, we would be alright. We need to cut out all this carnal and negative thinking, and start praying. Stop worrying about how God is going to work things out and who he is going to do it through. We are not smart enough to figure out God's plan. I don't know how he is going to bless me and I don't care as long as he blesses me. That is God's business. We are wondering how God is going to pay our bills and these bills that we have are nothing for God. There are many things that we are going to have to eliminate to have a free mind to concentrate on the things of God. That is when the anointing comes. God can then reveal things to our minds. If I can relieve my mind of my thinking, God can put thoughts of his will, in my mind; what God puts in my mind will take care of my thoughts.

I am reminded of the story of the two fish and the five loaves of bread. The people didn't have anything to eat and they just took the lunch of this little boy, gave it to Jesus and said that was all that they had. You may recall the story of how Jesus fed the five thousand with two fish and five loaves. As I read this story I received something. The little boy had to be willing to give up his lunch. He could have said, "NO!!, you cant have my lunch." Let me show you how Jesus works. He took that little boy's lunch and gave him twelve loaves in return. In Greek terminology, he had twelve *baskets* left over. Christ took his little paper bag lunch and gave him twelve baskets. His return was far greater than his gift. That is awesome. He gave up that little lunch that was just for that day, that lunch period, to get enough food to last him for breakfast, lunch, and dinner for that day and many more days as well. That is how the Lord work. Sometimes he takes the little that you have to give you an abundance. If you were to do research in this scripture, you will find that the twelve baskets that were left, were given to all those that were hungry. The natural mind wouldn't be able to comprehend this. It would think, "Why would God take my last?" He took his last to give him a plenty.

Things that we are not comfortable with keeps us from being happy. If you are not comfortable with people, you will not be happy even sitting beside them. Things around us has a big part to play in what we do, how we feel, react, talk, and look. We want to pray that we can master our surroundings.

There are other things that we feel that God haven't worked out yet. There are some things that we have to grow to, before it will be changed. There are some things that will not change, but that shouldn't discourage you because the God that you serve will let you know what he is going to change and what is going to remain the same. There is nothing to hard for him. But there are some things that Jesus and the apostles had to deal with, and we are going to have to deal with some things as well. There are some things that we can pray and pray about, and there will be a turn around. There are some things maybe you want changed tonight and it can be so, but a lot of times when *thing*s get changed so quickly and so easily, *we* don't change. That is why our sisters and brothers of the Old Testament had to go through trials and tribulations for so long. They didn't change. There are some things that will change when your talk changes. There are some that will automatically change when your thinking changes. There are some things that will change just as soon as the way you feel about them, changes. As soon as you stop getting mad, more things will change for you. God can change everything in your life, but he is not going to make you life perfect, when you don't do right. There are things that we are going to have to pray about, but as we pray, we are going to have to grow to receive them. There are many things that we *don't* have to pray about, because we know that we are already healed, delivered, and saved. As we pray for problems and situations to be worked out, (in some cases) there has to be a *working out* of the vessel that is praying. For example; we sometimes pray for a raise on the job. We ask God to touch the hearts of our bosses that they will give us a raise, but while we are on the job we are sitting down every chance we get. We forget that after we pray, God is still looking. We pray and ask God to give us another job and we are going to get on that job and do just what we were doing on our present job- nothing. There are some things that we have to get an understanding about, and then pray about. We must get an understanding of the bible. We are never alone. Jesus is always with us so we don't have any business praying, "Lord, I feel so lonely. I don't have any friends." The bible says that there is a friend that sticks closer than any brother. You are praying the wrong things. Prayers of this sort don't change, because you are praying against the book. There are some things that you may want in life, such as, wealth. What is wealth? Being rich in the spirit is wealth. Can you pray without praying in the right spirit? Sure you can. There are times we prayed one thing, and rose from our knees the same way we were when we first kneeled to pray. We want to eliminate those prayers.

St. Mark 11:24

Therefore I say unto you, What things soever you desire, when ye pray, believe that ye receive them, and ye shall have them.

We have to believe God to do whatever we have asked of him. He has the power to do all things. Jesus is talking to every one here. He is relaying the same thing to the poor as he is to the rich. There are people today who are afraid or reluctant to proclaim that they are rich in God. Did you know that death and life are in the power of the tongue? (Proverbs 18:21) That is , what you say out of your mouth. You have to speak with confidence, those things that you want to come to pass. You have to talk the way that you want things to actually be. We do not proclaim riches because we lack faith. Your life does not depend on the abundance of what you have. You cannot wait to get something to begin to talk. You have to talk when you don't have anything.

When you began to rise in the anointing of God, people may not be able to handle it. They don't have the understanding that you have. You have to ask God to rebirth the anointing in your life. When you rise up, people that are weak will not like it at all. Weak people like to be around weak people. People who have not experienced elevation, cannot appreciate elevation. People that are not obedient cannot appreciate people that are obedient. Even in a marriage, both spouses have to keep there spirits and anointing on the rise, because one can pull the other down. Husband and wife should be able to help each other. We have to be helpers one to another. You have to keep yourself straight to be able to help someone else.

Whatsoever things you desire:

This is pertaining to the things that you desire, and it does not matter what those things are. You have to pray to cover your desire, to make sure they are not lustful. You have to go to God in prayer and believe God for whatever your desire is. Everyone's desire is just as important as the next person's desire. Your desires should be wrapped up in your dreams. Your dream should be what you desire the most. There are times when you will not be able to share your desires with anyone. There are other times when you will be able to share them with someone. You have to let God lead you when it comes to sharing your desires with anyone. There should be something that you desire from God, even if it is only for a closer walk with him. Some of us allow our desires to run our lives, but we shouldn't. The things that you want from God should not be a burden to you , nor should it stress you out. If the word of God says that he will do it, then you can count it done. There are things that we desire but we don't go through the proper channels to obtain them. For everything that you desires there are principles that you must follow.

At times we look at other people and begin to desire things that they have. If you obey God and live right, he will bless you as well. The blessing of God will make you rich without adding sorrow

(Proverbs 10:22). You just have to use good, common sense with it. Your desire should be something that is in the will of God. Worldly wealth is what people desire most. Wealth that comes from God protects the soul from lusts that usually control people when they begin to increase in wealth. You should not ask God for something just for your personal use. What you desire should be something that from which God can get the glory. God is your life line. You have to continue to do what God has called you to do.

You have to be able to get a prayer through , to develop a relationship with God. There are many people who don't pray for their desires. When you pray, you have to believe that God has done what you asked of him, no matter how you feel. Even if the situation gets worse, you have to continue to believe God. You have to live by faith and not by your paycheck. God wants us to believe in him. If you desire a house, believe God and watch him come through for you. He will even bless you with the furnishings you need to go with the house. Pray, believe and watch God work. He will give you the desires of your heart.

St. Matthew 6:6

But thou, when thou prayest, enter into thy closet, and when thou hast shut thy door, pray to thy Father which is in secret; and thy Father which seeth in secret shall reward thee openly.

We, as people of God, are supposed to continually practice praying to God. It should be our duty. The scripture says *when*, thou prayest, because we do not pray often. When you pray, enter into your closet. Enter into a place of privacy. This is not particularly your natural closet, but the process of shutting out everything but you and God. He is our Father and he is ready and waiting to hear from us , and to answer our call. There are some prayers that are personal and you do not pray them in church.

You should only have one, ultimate father. You have to go to God in secret. There are some things that you will not be able to share with your spouse because they would not understand. Just because you are saved, does not mean that you are always going to be in harmony with everyone all the time.

God, your father will see you in secret and reward you openly.

Instead of praying to be seen of men, pray to God who is in secret. You are not to brag or boast when God blesses or rewards you. God is in your closet when no one else is there. He is there when you really need him and whenever you call upon him. When you pray openly for praise of man, you have already received your reward.

St. Matthew 6:7
But when ye pray use not vain repetitions, as the heathens do: for they think that they should be heard for their much speaking.

We do not impress God with a whole lot of lip-flapping. When you pray do not try to impress people by saying the same thing over and over or using big words. This, the bible says, is what the heathens do. A heathen is an unbeliever. We have a lot of heathens in the church world today. A heathen can be anyone who is not obedient. People love to hear themselves talk. If you do a lot of talking, you are only saying your prayer, you are not praying it.

St. Matthew 6:8
Be not ye therefore like unto them: for your Father knoweth what things you have need of, before you ask him.

We cannot be like the heathens. There are people that can pray for hours. They call these moving prayers. God already knows what you have need of before you ask him, so there is no need for an abundance of words. . When you pray, just go directly to the heart of the matter. Open your heart and just poor yourself out to God, and leave it there. God knows what we want and what we need , better than we know ourselves. After you have done this just thank the Lord and believe in him for what you have asked.

Philippians 4:6
Be careful for nothing; but in everything by prayer and supplication with thanksgiving let your request be made unto God.

We should pray about everything concerning our lives. When the scripture says be careful for nothing it means do not worry about anything but allow God to fix it. Pray to him so that he can ease our minds and lift our spirits, as well as give us direction and support. Getting upset, falling out, and rolling is not going to make the situation any better. Everything you do should have prayer in it. The very smallest thing to you, may be the largest thing to someone else. Sometimes before you open your mouth, you need to just pray.

Supplication

Supplication pertains to your attitude in your prayer. You can speak to God in a low tone of voice. It is not how loud you are but it is your faith in God that really moves him. The scripture says, thy faith hath made thee whole (St. Matthew 9:22). Veronica's faith is what made her whole, not the fact that she pressed her way through the crowd. She said, "If I could but touch the hem of his garment, I know that I will be made whole." You know that faith cometh by hearing and hearing by the word of God.

Think about a spirit of thanksgiving. You must join a spirit of thanksgiving with your prayers. When people look at you, they should see that spirit in you, not a spirit that would make them ask what is wrong with you. You cannot have anything against other people when you pray.

Let your request be made known unto God.

When you pray, you are offering up your desires to the Lord. Talk to God and let him know what your request is: not that he needs to be told, but because he wants to hear them from us. Most of our talk needs to be directed in prayer. We have a tendency to talk about things that we shouldn't. You have to release those things that you do not like, in prayer.

Philippians 4:7
And the peace of God, which passeth all understanding, shall keep your hearts and minds through Christ Jesus.

Once you do all of the above, the peace of God will come and you will not worry yourself to death. It will keep our hearts and minds through Christ Jesus, and it will help us not to faint while we are going through our trials and tribulations. Believe that it will happen. The peace of God will give you the understanding to relax, and consider it done.

There is no way that you can serve a God that you can't pray to. That lets me know that there are a lot of people who are not serving God but are serving the devil, because they don't pray to God.

St. Mark 1:35
And in the morning, rising up a great while before day, he went out and departed into a solitary place, and there he prayed

Jesus here was giving us an example of a secret prayer. There are times that you have to go into a secret prayer because if people knew what you are praying about, they would try to hinder your prayer. Sometimes you will have to get up before daybreak to pray. When our spirits are the freshest and most alert, is when we should do our praying. Sometimes you may be in an awkward position and every one else is home sleeping, but get your prayer in. Sometimes God will lead you to a secret place. The devil sits around and listens to your prayers and then he tries to hinder them, and to keep them from being answered.

A solitary place represents a lonely place where you are by yourself. When it comes to God you are never alone (Hebrews 13:5). There will be times when you will have to go into a solitary place to get away from people. A time to have some alone time for just you and God. There are times when people will listen to your prayers and take them the wrong way.

When you pray, be honest with God. Let him know that you are not where you should be. You may have to get by yourself to say a prayer like such: "Lord, the devil really used me today", or "Lord I am tired of this demon that causes me to get mad or upset about every little thing." Sometimes you will have to get by yourself and just empty out to God. Let him know that you are hardheaded and don't want to listen to anyone. When you go to God in secret, that is your opportunity to get really serious with him. Ask him to forgive you of all of your sins. Let God know that you do not take things well and that you always allow your feelings to get hurt. Ask him to save you from all of your sins. Ask him to save you from your old self, and from acting like momma and daddy. Ask God not to let you hold things against other people. Ask him not to let you smile and grin in peoples faces when you actually have something against them in your heart. God already knows how we are. Just ask him to save you so you won't be left behind when he comes to take his children home. You don't want him to come and catch you with your work undone.

You don't have to worry about God taking your prayer wrong. Man will take it wrong and use it against you, but God knows exactly what you are trying to say. You have to pray to develop a relationship with God. When you pray, ask him to create within you a clean heart and to renew that right spirit within you (Psalms 51:10). You have to be wise enough to get yourself right when you are alone so that God won't have to openly rebuke or correct you in the church. Then you won't be getting mad with the preacher. They are only the messengers.

Ephesians 6:18
Praying always with all prayer and supplication in the spirit, and watching thereunto with all perseverance and supplication for all saints.

We are focusing on another type of prayer now. This is a command or duty, prayer that we are all supposed to pray. Although we don't do it enough, this prayer will take you out of yourself (flesh) and put you in a praying spirit. Often times this type of prayer is not made because it has to be done in the spirit. This is a prayer for those individuals who have held on and who have kept the spirit of God. The very thing that you ask for should be in accordance to the scripture. It should line up with the scripture. This scripture only applies to the believer that is in the spirit, for only the believer that is in the spirit, can pray in the spirit. You have to pray and watch, in the spirit.

Perseverance only means to continue. We must continue praying for as long as we live. At times it will seem like things that you have prayed for, isn't going to happen, but just continue; it will happen. You are doubtful at times, but if God said it, it will come to pass. When perseverance is in action, it does not stop or get dismayed, it keeps right on praying. Supplication has to be made for every believer. Not for ourselves only, but for every believer. You have to pray for people when they are not even praying for themselves. Everyone's job should be to witness to people and to win souls for God.

St John 17:1-26

This chapter elaborates on the prayer that Jesus prayed to his Father. Throughout his entire prayer, Jesus did not include the devil anywhere. He did not give him credit for anything. When you do not do what God tells you to do the substitute steps in. This substitute is the devil. If you do what God tells you to do, you will gain victory. Your focus will not be on anything that the devil has done. If you are not doing what God says do, then you are doing what the devil says.

I Kings 8:33-39

33. When thy people Israel be smitten down before the enemy, because they have sinned against thee, and shall turn again to thee, and confess thy name, and pray, and make supplication unto thee in this house:

34. Then hear thou in heaven, and forgive the sin of thy people Israel, and bring them again unto the land which thou gavest unto their fathers.

35. When heaven is shut up and there is no rain, because they have sinned against thee; if they pray toward this place, and confess thy name, and turn from their sin, when thou afflictest them:

36. Then hear thou in heaven, and forgive the sin of thy servants, and of thy people Israel, that thou teach them the good way wherein they should walk, and give rain upon thy land, which thou hast given to thy people for an inheritance.

37. If there be in the land famine, if there be pestilence, blasting, mildew, locust, or if there be caterpillar; if their enemy besiege them in the land of their cities; whatsoever plague, whatsoever sickness there be;

38. What prayer and supplication soever be made by any man, or by all thy people Israel, which shall know every man the plague of his own heart, and spread forth his hand toward this house:
39. Then hear thou in heaven thy dwelling place, and forgive, and do, and give to every man according to his ways, whose heart thou knowest; (for thou, even thou only, knowest the hearts of all the children of men;)

The people lost what they were supposed to have because they sinned. Their prayer would not be answered until they turned from their sins. When they asked for forgiveness God forgave them. You have to have a repentance prayer. A repentance prayer is a prayer in which you repent of all your sins. Most of the times we are repenting for things we didn't do, not things that we have done. We should pray that God would teach us the way in which we should walk, by his spirit and with his word.

Exhorted Prayer

St. Luke 18:10-12
10. Two men went up into the temple to pray; the one a Pharisee, and the other a publican.
11. The Pharisee stood and prayed thus with himself, God, I thank thee, that I am not as other men are, extortioners, unjust, adulterers, or even as this publican.
12. I fast twice in the week, I give tithes of all that I possess.

In this scripture, we find that the Pharisee was esteeming himself above the other people. He was praying a very selfish prayer. He began his prayer by telling God what he had done. He started bringing out the good things that he had done. He told so much that he began to brag on himself. His purpose was to show off for the people and to make himself look good. He really had not done anything great. He had done what he was supposed to do. There are many people in church today that do things to be seen of men. These very people will lose out in judgement day. You cannot feel like you are better than people because there is something wrong with them. We all have some type of habit, whether it is just talking too much or just thinking evil. This is why you cannot think that you are better than any one else.

St. Luke 18:13

And the publican, standing afar off, would not lift up so much as his eyes unto heaven, but smote upon his breast, saying, God be merciful to me, a sinner.

The publican was praying a very sorrowful prayer. He felt as though he was not worthy. He was very humble. He came to the temple to make his request known unto God. His prayer was full of humility. When it comes to God's power, we are nothing. God can wave his hand and we will be finished. You cannot be high minded or exalted. You have to develop a prayer life in which you are humble.

The publican acknowledged who he was and where he was in life, in his prayer. When you ask God to be merciful unto you, that is acknowledging him. You are letting him know just where you are. We are depending on the mercy of God.

St. Luke 18:14

I tell you, this man went down to his house justified rather than the other: for every one that exalteth himself shall be abased; and he that humbleth himself shall be exalted.

The publican here was justified because he was honest and truthful. He did not pray like he had never done anything wrong. This is the same way we have to be. When you pray to God, be humble. Just ask God to help you. Did you know that you can take the things of God out of proportion? You have to pay your tithes and fast. If you do not fast, you will remain the same. If you do not pay your tithes, you will always find yourself broke. When you go to God you have to approach him humbly.

An individual can only exalt themselves when they brag about what they are doing. You will say, "I did all of this by myself, no one came to help me." If you are a good and lovable person, someone else will be able to tell it. If God has blessed you, you won't have to blow your own trumpet.

An humble person can handle being exalted. When an humble person is exalted, they remain humble. When an humble person reaches the mountain top they will meditate on what they can do to help others.

Hypocritical prayer

Job 27:8-9

8. For what is the hope of the hypocrite, though he hath gained, when God taketh away his soul?

9. Will God hear his cry when trouble cometh upon him?

A hypocrite is a person who just goes to church. Often times they never get right, they just go. They appear to be one thing when they are actually something else. Their entire prayer is bless me God, do this God, do that God.

When God takes away your soul, you wont have anything. Because people are blessed, they feel like God hears their prayers. Most hypocritical people pray for natural or material things all the time. You are considered to be hypocritical when your mind is constantly on natural things and never on spiritual things. You are also hypocritical when you teach and tell people what is in the bible and you are not obeying it yourself.

The question is, will God hear your cry. He will not hear your cry unless true repentance has taken place. Unless there is a change, God will not find favor in you. You have to be very careful. Why should God heal you for you to continue to serve the devil? God hears prayers of repentance. When an individual really desires to make a change, God is able to recognize their sincere prayer. Do not pray a hypocritical prayer. God will not hear you.

Prayer of neglect

Proverbs 28:9

He that turneth away his ear from hearing the law, even his prayer shall be abomination.

Sometimes people pray but they neglect God's law. God speaks to us by his law, and he expects us to listen and take heed. When you turn away from the law, which is God's word, he will not hear your prayer. Your prayer is no good when you fail to obey the word. Excuses will not work with God. There are so many things that we desire from God, but we fail to obey his word. All we want Is God's goods. You cannot neglect God's word and try to pray your way through. You have to obey his word so that he will hear your prayer and you can wait for an answer..

Prayer of iniquity

Isaiah 59:2-6

2. But your iniquities have separated between you and your God, and your sins have hid his face from you, that he will not hear.

3. For your hands are defiled with blood, and your fingers with iniquity; your lips have spoken lies; your tongue have muttered perverseness.

4. None calleth for justice, nor any pleadeth for truth: they trust in vanity, and speak lies; they conceive mischief, and bring forth iniquity.

5. They hatch cockatrice' eggs, and weave the spider's web: he that eateth of her eggs dieth, and that which is crushed breaketh out into a viper.

6. Their webs shall not become garments, neither shall they cover themselves with their works: their works are works of iniquity, and the act of violence is in their hands.

A prayer of iniquity is a dangerous prayer. Sin will keep good things from you. No one really knows that it is an iniquity prayer but you. It is a hidden prayer: one that you will never tell. Sin will hide God's face from you. Sin puts you in position where God doesn't want to see you. It hides the mercy of God, and erects a wall between you and him. It is bad when you are testifying, preaching and singing and God does not want to see you. Sin separates you from every good thing that you could have. God loves you so, that he turns his head away from you. God will turn his face and not even hear your prayer. We often mess up and declare to to God, that he is a God of a second chance.

Sometimes you put your lipstick or your chapstick on and your lips are still talking lies. Your words pretend to be kind, when they are actually meant to cause harm. Perverseness relates to the way you actually tell things. You can build up what you are talking about and cause someone else to be messed up. These things bring forth sin. We have to be watchful of them. We are always praying for God to help us, and he is *always* helping us. You have to receive your help while it is being given. Remind yourself that sin, when it is finished, will bring only death.

Jeremiah 14:10-12

10. Thus saith the Lord unto this people, Thus have they learned to wander, they have not refrained their feet, therefore the Lord doth not except them; he will now remember their iniquity, and visit their sins.

11. Then said the Lord unto me, Pray not for this people for their good.

12. When they fast, I will not hear their cry; and when they offer burnt offering and an oblation, I will not except them: but I will consume them by the sword, and by the famine, and by the pestilence.

God talks to his people. In this verse of scripture, he says, "*this* people" because they had broken covenant with him. When people love to wander, they cannot be stationary. They have reverted to the things they were doing first. They are people who proclaim the name of Jesus but they do not do the things the bible say do. When you do not do what God says to do, he will not except you. Therefore

God does not accept anything. He will withdraw from you. God does not accept everything running around saying hallelujah. God will remember how you lived and the things you have done. God is coming to see us about our sins, not our faithful work in the church. You cannot make it unless you rectify your sins.

II Chronicles 7:14

If my people, which are called by name, shall humble themselves, and pray, and seek my face, and turn from their wicked ways; then will I hear from heaven, and will forgive their sin, and will heal their land.

This scripture pertains to the church. This scripture is dealing with prayer, and everyone should have a prayer of humility. A prayer of humility is a prayer in which you always see yourself, instead of the other person. It is a prayer that allows God to deal with you.

Do you really belong to God?

When you are acting crazy, foolish, and suffering trials and tribulations, and your body is not what it is supposed to be, do you belong to him? No matter what you are going through you still belong to God. There are some things you can change when you recognize who you belong to.

We have to humble ourselves in prayer. Humility is not based on your talk. A humility prayer is one that helps us to develop a relationship with God. Have you ever gone to God and you were at one level but you were supposed to be higher? You know that you have not mistreated anyone. You know that you have been obedient, yet you are not where you are supposed to be. Most often people get along good until they make up there minds to please and serve the Lord. Then demons from everywhere try to bombard your vessel. When things come in on you, that is the time that you have to use your power.

Most of the time when we have a problem or situation, we tell God about it. But we have to turn it around and tell the situation about God. Let the problem or situation know that God said thus and so. You are a child of the King. God also said that he would not put any more on you than you can bare. You are the head and not the tail. Continue to tell your spirit that you are the head and not the tail.

The word themselves mean that everyone consisting of the entire individual or the whole being. The word themselves let's me know that I am not always myself. There are times when we act like someone else: that is not ourselves. You know that you do not generally holler at people like you have done, that is not you. You have to come to grips with who you really are. Sometimes you are who God has called you to be. Then there are times when you are who your parents named you. That is the part that you have to come to grips with. There are times when we do not act like who God made us. Sometimes the image of ourselves show up in other people. The very thing that you cannot stand is what he or she will do. What you have to do is turn that around. God has to use someone to get that high-mindedness, boastfulness, and lying out of you. He wants to get all that other stuff out so his will, will be the only thing in you. Sometimes when you get up in the morning, and someone asks what's the matter with you, your response is, "oh, I am fine." You know that you are not really fine. You just tell them what they want to hear to get them out of your face.

There are so many handicapped spirits that lurk in our vessels. A lot of times we do not realize it but the spirit of God is moving in one area in us and something else is moving in another area. You have to pray to get those spirits out of you. Pray, "Lord humble me so that I will not fly off on people." There are some people who are humble and quiet, but sometimes you just have to tell people what is right, whether they like it or not. There are some things that will not get any better until you stand up and be the man or woman of God that you are supposed to be. There is a time and a season for everything. There is a time to take the humble approach, and there are the times to know this will not happen again. There are some things that you have to take a stand on. There are times when you will have to be a floor mat, and there are times when you cannot be a floor mat.

Seeking God's face is something we do not do very often unless we want something. And when you seek God it is not in faith. Once you get to the place where you can say, "Lord the things that I am telling and thinking now are not right," then you can discover the face of the Lord. We know God's make up and he does not act like the devil. You seek the face of God by knowing what his word says. God is meek and lowly in heart. You are not lowly in heart being stupid or being a bully. You have to learn to be a peacemaker. There are some things you just do not want to hear.

Turning from our wicked ways, is the part that is most difficult for us to do. It is hard for some people to let things go. Most people will let it go and then go and pick it back up again. You have to turn away from the things that God has delivered you from. You have to turn away from the way you used to act. It is not easy to turn away from some of your old ways. It is not easy to be a new creature. Life presents itself to bring stuff back to you. Can you think of something that you have turned away from since you have been in the church? Have you "dabbed" in it since you turned away?

CHAPTER FIVE:
DON'T LET THE ADVERSARY
HINDER YOUR RELATIONSHIP
WITH GOD

There is a feeling that will never leave you. On your best days it will be there. You have to reach the point where you can declare that, it's not by feeling nor by sight. Sometimes you can't see that things are shaping up, but be assured that the just shall live by faith, and every thing that God has promised you, believe that your faith is enough if you stand on that solid rock called Jesus. The devils job is to get you to doubt God and he uses what is already yours to make you do so. Whatever God has told you he would do, he will bring it to pass. Don't doubt, give up, or accept a substitute. Believe that God can give you the real thing, even though at times things don't seem to be working out. He can take nothing and make something beautiful out of it. Stand on his word. Delight yourself in God and not in man. Man will hurt your feelings and cause walls to build up in you. . Delight yourself in God and he will give you the desires of your heart. The desires are waiting on you. Some desires you are not ready for. Every desire that you receive, causes you to grow up a little more in the Lord. Sometimes it costs you something. Every desire depends upon you. God doesn't fix anything for you, just so that you can remain the same. Sometimes God is *waiting* to bless us. We have to grow to our blessings. He doesn't make kindergarten students, immediate professors. We have to grow up to receive a blessing from the Lord. There are things that cause a delay. You can get to the door and the door is wide open, but hypocrisy, lying, backbiting, and such will hinder you from walking through. Only the pure in heart can walk into blessings. The door can be wide open, but my character has a lot to do with whether I make it through the door or not.

We have to discover the way we are, check yourself. Take inventory of your life: the way you handle things, your reactions, your feelings, your character, your thoughts, etc. We have to fall out of love with the way we are. None but the righteous shall see God.

If I don't change the way that I am, I can't handle some of the blessings that God is ready to give me. Stop dwelling on the blessings and dwell on God. Say unto him, God I want to please you and walk upright with you. We say this and then we do nothing but sit down. Don't let this be the case for you. Once I realize that the image in me is not the one suitable for God's blessings, I have to make haste and correct this image so that I can receive the blessings of God. There is nothing poor about God, so there shouldn't be anything poor about me. Sometimes God will give you blessings and watch you walk around and talk about the blessings on your job; but you add to the blessings or take away from them.

We are living in the last days and everything that was wrong with you , you are already supposed to have given it to God. The thing is, we are living in times where we are dealing with a *modern* devil. A new age devil. We have to deal with the devil in a new way. You must start with yourself. You may be saved and beautiful, but you have to tell yourself what God said you are to be, and you must be just that. Tell yourself what God said about you, the potential he sees in you, the life he desires you to have, and the blessings he has in store, and make yourself understand that you will be exactly what God said you are to be. You have to be strong. Turn things around. We have to turn it around, instead of telling God to do something for me that *I* am supposed to do, I need to do it for myself. You have cried on God's shoulder. Destiny is in your hands. God told you to love regardless. You may not want to love, but you have to for your problems or situations to be solved. God works them out and he works you out at the same time. No one in the bible was delivered and remained the same. When God does something for you, you have to change along with what God has done. We have to turn thing around and stop telling God, but tell the problem what God said. Change the situation. Tell yourself that God doesn't have any sneaky, cunning people. Tell yourself that God's people are lovely, kind and sober, and this is the way we have to be if we are going to make it to heaven.

We are a people that despises chastisement or correction. You wont have to be chastized or rebuked if you would chastize yourself. You will never be caught in wrong. Every body says that they love God. How can I have a plroblem with someone and still say I love God? I can't. How can I say I love God and I don't love you. We have to believe God. If we believe, it will shape and mold us into what we are supposed to be. Then I can see how to help my sister or brother. The adversary is not in my sister or brother but is in me. It has to be in me to make me dislike you or have funny felings against you. I can't talk about you unless the enemy has gotten into me. There is no way that I can get upset about your work for God unless the enemy has gotten into me. I am supposed to love, regardless. There lis no way that I can break friendship with you unless the enemy has gotten into me. God loves the church and Jesus loved it so that he gave his life for the church. How can I get upset with the church unless the devil is in me. There is no way that I can get upset with you when you are doing everything you can to make God's ministry grow unless the adversary is in me.

Lucifer was in heaven and he got mad with God because he was jealous of him. When people get jealous of you they will put you down. Make up in your mind that you will give them something to talk about. I'm going to keep love in my heart no matter what goes on. Keep your eyes on the adversary. It is the adversary that brings the trouble, not your brother or sister. God is not the author of confusion. When two can't see eye to eye, the adversary has entered one or both of you. The devil is the adversary. He doesn't always get into people, he can get into your circumstances and tear you apart. You can have five children that don't give you any problems, but that sixth child is the one that the devil uses to get the best of you.

Everything that looks good, is not good. Example: Before you were saved you may have had a woman or man that appeared good looking on the outside but they turned out to be bad to the bone. The devil uses whatever he can to tear up things, but you have to discover who or what he is in. All unrighteousness is sin. The enemy will get into different things to take you out. He comes only to kill, steal, and destroy. Something may be going on for years and years and you can get by but, the devil may be using it to build his cage. The devil will continue to talk to your mind. When your mind is messed up, it is hard to get it back. The devil will get into things and start pushing. He will get into both hands. He will tell the left hand that the right hand needs to apologize, and vice versa.

We have too many if's and but's in us that is why we can't serve God. When God first saved you, there no if's and but's.

Do you see yourself and the devil in you. It's your job to see Jesus and it's the Pastors job to deal with what goes on. The enemy gets into things to conquer and divide. He is out to tear things up. Most people allow the devil to mess them up, and they in turn mess up everything around them. You have argued with your brothers and sisters not knowing that the devil was in it from the beginning. You have to be what God says you are to be, or you will suffer.

It's time for us to get up and be what God has called us to be. The main job of the adversary is to keep you from making heaven your home. He wants you to be left out like he will be. You will be looking for daddy and mamma and they will be gone. The devil is out to keep you fighting with your sisters and bothers because he knows that you can't win souls to Christ if you yourself are fighting. You can't be lazy and expect someone else to build up what you are supposed to be building. We have to get busy doing what we are supposed to be doing in Christ.

Sin will break your fellowship with God. All of these habits that we have: lying, being deceitful, etc., we have to get rid of. Most of the saints today have lost the joy and excitement that they once had. Back in the day people had that agape love and we know that love will move the spirit. Our love is not in operations the way God desires for it to be. When you have the genuine love you will not feel anything. Do you know that because of iniquity sins, the love of many have waxed cold? Most of the people who have a problem loving, do not love themselves. When an individual loves himself they will not have a problem loving the next person. Now days even in the church a person can be your buddy but when things begin to happen they will separate themselves. When you forgiver you are supposed to forget.

CHAPTER SIX:
EVALUATING YOUR PROGRESS IN GOD

We need to know that God does not see us as we see ourselves.

II Corinthians 5:17
Therefore if any man be in Christ, he is a new creature: old
things are passed away; behold, all things are become new.

Sometimes it might seam like you are not doing anything but in the eyesight of God, you are still moving on. Some times we go through a dry season, but look at what you *could* be doing. You could be doing drugs, alcohol, etc. Your walk with God has to be constant. You have to remember that you are in Christ. Don't let the devil detour your thinking from Christ. Don't let him destroy your confidence in Christ. Remember that the blood of Christ, covered your mistakes. Everything that you do is covered under the blood. God loves us enough to reveal the things about us that are not like him. This is only giving us another chance to correct them. Your flaws will take away your strength if you allow them. The devil uses them to keep tripping you up. The things that stopped you last year should not be able to stop you this year. Say to yourself, "(call your name), I repented of this last year and I am not going to let this situation get in my way this year. Flaws will weigh you down. Your flaws also are good for you in the sense that they let you know that you still need God. The flaws reveal unto us what we still need to work on. What we need to do to make us better and blesses us even more, not hurt us. It gets you closer to God and makes you more like Christ.

The devil will have you not to know whether you are in or out of Christ. You have to make the choice, that you are in. You may not be perfect, you may have came up short, but you are in Christ. People are afraid to confess their faults in fear that people will tell it. This causes you to keep it to yourself, but you have to let it go. You might not have shaped up in the eyesight of man but man cannot stop you if you don't allow him. Strive to please God, not man. You can't get around the word. If you want to please God, you must be found in the word of God.

In Christ you are saved and don't allow what people are saying about you, stop you from being saved. How people feel about you should'nt stop you. We have one judge and if we please him, what man says does not matter. It can't stop you from going to heaven.

You must realize that you are serving God for yourself. We fall out of this race because of other people. Your goal should be to please God and God alone. Don't give up and stop attending church. Everyone is trying to make it in.

Your newness in God has to be clarified in you. You have to know that your spirit is new beyond a shadow of doubt. You must know that you are a new creature. You have come short but you are still a new creature. This does not mean that you will do everything right. You do better as you learn. At times we do wrong when we know better, but sometimes you don't have the strength or power to overcome in that area. You must ask God to help you over come or deliver you in that area. This still doesn't mean that I am not a new creature.

Romans 5:3

And not only so, but we glory in tribulations also: knowing that tribulations worketh patience;

Paul here is talking about things we go through when we are saved. Tribulations are things that you go through that you really don't deserve to go through, but you don't change and act like the devil while you are going through them. Patience could do us more good than tribulation can do us hurt. It's tribulation to the believer when you are going through something and you know that you didn't do anything to deserve this, but you kept yourself together. You didn't mouth off at that brother or sister, you held your peace.

You can never tell people what you really want to tell them or you will be out of the will of God. You can only talk to a certain extent. It's helping you to learn and endure.

WORKETH PATIENCE

These things help you to shut your mouth, stop flipping out, stop acting unseemly, and drive you to the point where you will get patience. Sometimes we do things before we think. Patience wasn't in play. We take matters into our own hands because we don't have patience. You can't make anybody do anything. Tribulations brings you to the point where you can have patience. Always remember that I am saved and I am a new creature and it will bring you back to your senses and help you hold your peace. When you retaliate it makes you look as guilty as the other person. People will focus on you and say that you are supposed to be the saved one.

Patience worketh experience, with the devil, troubles, and your own failures. This happened for ten years and I am not going to fall apart this time. When you have weakness, counteract them with something else to keep it from happening again. If you have a problem getting mad, sing a song, do something to keep yourself from getting mad.

If we rebel against what God is saying, he will do us like he did Paul. Paul tried to fight against God. He said it is hard to kick against the prick. When God finished with him he was a changed man.

Experience worketh hope. Hope assures you of yourself. You have to live so that you can be sure. You have to know that you are on the right track. You obtain hope by learning from your experiences. When it happens again, you have hope. The hope we have by serving God. The love of God is what brings you out. Don't let people get to you even when you are wrong. I can go to God if I go to the person and get it right, just don't do it again. That will teach you too. You have to wise up. You obtain more experience when you go through things and you are able to take it. His spirit keeps you from falling. If you take matters into your own hands you will feel bad because you have left the will of God. The Holy Ghost is given unto us. It takes over when you go through. It sustains you. When the Holy Ghost is operating in you, you want to do things and can't do it. You want to retaliate but you can't retaliate. The Holy Ghost has then taken over. When we were yet without strength (before you got saved, you were weak), Christ died for you to give you strength so you can be delivered from your sins. He died to make you strong so the things you used to do, you don't do them anymore. You have to have some direction. I onced had a problem smoking but now I am set free. There is no need for me to go gazing at a cigarette or it will get in my spirit and I will be smoking again. When God deliver you, say to yourself, this is the very thing that God delivered me from and I am going to stay away from that. Never think that you are so strong that satan can't tempt you. You are no stronger than the people you hang around. Hang around good people, they will help strengthen you. The world will pull you back. You can be a preacher but it can still pull you back. If you know that you had a problem being sneaky, then you can't hang around with sneaky people. Your old habits are still lingering and when you get around that stuff it works on you and takes affect on you. Keep in mind no matter what, I am a new creature and what you think of me is not going to revert me to the old creature. . You have a new spirit and a will to do new things (things of God). You can only do right as you learn. You have to learn how to love God and obey him. We can't love him until we read his word and learn of what he requires of us.

Old things are passes away.

I am going to let them stay away. I am not going to do anything to bring them back. Your lifestyle will change. You won't have to prove anything to people, they will know. If they see you doing the same thing again that gives them the opportunity to say you are not saved and you haven't changed. You are then representing the old creature. Sometimes we get relaxed and playful. That is the closest thing to the old you there is. You may be talking about things that you are not supposed to be talking about and someone will be listening and get offended. They are not looking for you to be playing, joking or acting like that. I can laugh and talk without getting the conversation out of the will of God. You never know who is listening to your conversation. The saints get relaxed and play and act up with each other and say they are saved. People have watched you act up. Always handle things as a new creature in Christ would, because you never know when someone is listening. Be saved everywhere you go. You have to stop so much laughing and talking. If you have to stop your conversation when you see the man or woman of God approaching, then you know that your conversation was wrong and out of the will of God. You are behaving in a way that you are not supposed to behave. On any job, you have to act like a new creature. You have to do the same at home as well. Some of us are nice and kind in church but when we get home you have to wonder what is going on with us. You have to be the same every where you go. Every believer has to carry himself the same way.

All things are become new

All things will become new once God cover all of my old deeds. I want to know everything I can know about the Lord so that if anything is wrong, I can stop it. Our mind also becomes new. You have the old ways down packed, now you want to learn the new ways of Christ. Everyone will know your old ways but because you are different now, you will handle things in a different way. Because you are new, you don't act that way anymore. You have to carry yourself as a saved man or woman or you will turn people off. You can't act like a child one minute and try to act in your given title the next . People are looking to see something in you that isn't right so that they can use it against you down the road. Everything you do should be of God. God is going to be right and ,every man a liar. When you do things that are not of God you are messing up. This is what brings about the fall. Your sin will put you down because you are worried to death about something, and people don't even know.

We have to help each other. What I done yesterday, don't hold it against me today. Let's not put each other down. This is how you get yourself going and how you become new. Forget what happened in the past. If you have sincerely repented, then forget it. Start over and be all you can be in God. Start today and do all that you know is right to do. God will mature you when you do that. My walk with God will return when I do what I am supposed to do each day. My anointing also comes back when I am doing what I am supposed to do.

Don't let your surroundings pull you down. If you let your guard down your surroundings will pull you down from the standard that you are supposed to be lifting for God. Be careful around a group of people who are playing and acting up, they will bring you down. Hold up your standard. If I am a women of God who plays every day, then you won't respect me. Some people in church get in a routine of doing things and don't realize that a new soul has come into the church and they are watching you and judging you. Try to better yourself and watch how people will try to bring you down. You are judged in your neighborhood and on your job. All I have to do is come to your neighborhood to know how saved you are. People will tell on you so you have to do right all the time. If they see you doing something wrong, the whispering will travel all up and down the street. Be saved everywhere you go. Even dealing with your family you have to be saved. When your family gets mad at you for doing right, that is a good thing. When they began to talk about things that you are doing that are not right, then that is bad.

Holding on to hurt

If you want to get over hurt and heal old wounds, just think about how much dirt you have done and watch how quick you get over them. Tell yourself that this person haven't done any more to you than you have done to someone else.

The first thing the devil tries to do when you go to church is to get you hurt by someone in the church, in hope you will leave. No one can really hurt you unless you allow yourself to be hurt. If I have done something to you, I will get it right with you, I will not walk around with that hurt. No one can stop you from serving God and no one can stop you from feeling his spirit. I stop the spirit of God when I have done wrong. Obey God and his spirit will flow. His joy and anointing will also flow in your life. As you learn of God, keep his commandments. Do those things that are according to his will, and you will continue to make progress in him. Do these things and watch how much closer your relationship with God will be.

CHAPTER SEVEN:
REJOICE IN YOUR RELATIONSHIP WITH GOD

You cannot praise God until you have on a spiritual garment of praise. When the garment of praise is upon you, it will be all down on the inside of your vessel. It will show up any where. You are supposed to enter into the house of God uplifted. You are not supposed to come into the church down and depressed. When you do not keep your mind on God, you will not have a desire to praise him.

To maintain and perceive this garment of praise, you cannot lie, cheat, or steal, and expect a garment of praise to be present. God has never moved you into a realm in him, that you cannot praise him. One has to maintain goodness and the will of God, in order to possess a garment of praise. How many people do we have in the church world today that *really* want to praise God?

You have to concentrate on God all day to maintain a garment of praise. Natural things have taken over our praise. We tend to spend more time thinking on and worrying about bills, cars, homes, clothes, shoes, what we are going to do tomorrow, kids, spouse, etc. The natural things are not supposed to take anything away from us spiritually. You cannot meditate and concentrate on God and run your mouth, or get upset, at the same time. We are doing too many other things to do the job that we are required to do.

It is imperative that you have a garment of praise in order to develop a relationship with God.

Prasies does several things:

Brings you into God's glory

Shuts the enemy out

When you have God on your mind and you are in his presence the enemy has to get back. Never get so complacent and believe that God *really* has to do something for you. *You* have to do something for God, so that he will be able to heal, deliver, and set you free. We need God so badly that we have to make the first effort to get him.

Sin will break your fellowship with God and you will not have the joy and excitement that God intended for you to have.

I Corinthians 13:6

Rejoiceth not in iniquity, but rejoiceth in the truth;

You have to recognize and know what takes away your joy and your dance. You are not supposed to rejoice in iniquity: in doing harm and mischief. When you *know* that you are wrong, you are not supposed to rejoice. You do not rejoice in or entertain sin, whether it is known or hidden. You have to stop being partaker of those things that you know are not right, or you *are* rejoicing in iniquity. You are only supposed to rejoice in truth.

No matter what comes your way, you can rejoice because victory is already yours. You have developed a relationship with God now. He will never fail you or let you down.

Since I have a relationship with him now, I realize that a delay is not a denial. Although God delays on some things, he does not deny. He will show up. You can feel good about your relationship because you know that all things are working together for your good (Romans 8:28). We as believers suffer many things, but the spirit God will be there to intercede and intervene for us. When tears are running down your face, God will wipe them away. Because you have established a relationship with God, you know that weeping may endure for a night, but joy will come in the morning (Psalms 30:5). Sometimes you have to make joy come. Whatever God says it should be, that is what it will be. God said that sadness and mourning shall flee. If God is able to do that, why are you mourning and depressed? Do you remember the widow woman? She wanted something and she did not get it right away, but she kept going back until she got just what she wanted from God.

You have got to let your soul magnify the Lord.

I know for a fact that you cannot dance until you do right. One has to discover what produces joy and what impairs joy. When you dance, that represents that you have passed over or defeated the problem. The dance represents that you have overcome. Moses and the Israelites had to cross the red sea before they could dance. Moses had to do right before the red sea would even divide. After they crossed the red sea, Miriam got a tambourine and began to dance before the Lord.

Exodus 18:9-10

9. And Jethro rejoiced for all the goodness which the Lord had done to Israel, whom he had delivered out of the hands of the Egyptians.

10. And Jethro said, Blessed be the Lord, who hath delivered you out of the hands of the Egyptians, and out of the hand of Pharaoh, who hath delivered the people from under the hands of the Egyptians.

Jethro rejoiced for all God's goodness. He not only rejoiced for what was done for his son-in- law, but he rejoiced for all of the goodness done to all of Israel. That is reason enough alone to rejoice in the Lord. Without God, you can't rejoice. God has delivered some of us from the clubs, the casino, the whorehouses, the race track, the street corners, etc. He delivered you from spending and wasting all your money. Let your mind wander back and think on the things that God has delivered you from. Those are reasons that you have the right and the duty to rejoice in him. This is just one benefit of developing a relationship with him.

Psalms 28:7-9

7. The Lord is my strength and my shield; my heart trusteth in him, and I am helped: therefore my heart greatly rejoiceth; and with my song will I praise him.

8. The Lord is their strength, and he is the saving strength of his anointed.

9. Save thy people, and bless thine inheritance: feed them also, and lift them up forever.

God is the strength of every believer. He is our help. We have a reason to trust, believe and depend on him because he has already done countless things for us and on our behalf. He is helping us not to go back to those things we used to do, those places we used to go, and those feelings we used to have. Doesn't that make your heart rejoice? It should because it was God that kept you from fainting while you were going through theses things. Your whole body should rejoice. Praise God in your song. Your song might not be someone else's song, but you praise him with the song that is down in your soul.

The Lord is your strength and he is the saving strength of your anointing. He is that strength that breaks every yoke. It's the strength of his anointing. Some people may think they are too young and that they have to "catch up", but there is no age in God. Anyone that desires to do so may have his anointing. What he says to one, he says to all.

Luke 1:47

And my spirit hath rejoiced in God my Savior

You don't know what the outcome of your situation is going to be. If I were you, I would say to my spirit, "You *will* rejoice." Mary proclaimed that her soul rejoiced in God because of the good things he had done for her. She realized that she was pregnant and she said that she would rejoice, because she *knew* that God was doing a good thing. God had chosen her to do the honor of bringing the Messiah, the savior of all mankind, into this world. This honor that he gave her is one that will last forever. At times, we will go through trials and tribulations, but you have to tell yourself, that no matter how it looks, you will rejoice. These trials and tribulations think they have you captive, but tell your spirit, you will rejoice. Life and death is in the tongue. It is time to rejoice when it looks like you are at the end of the line.

Mary knew what was happening to her and she said that God had done her a great thing. He is too mighty to make a mistake. She held God up. You have to dwell in the spirit. You can't hold him up in the flesh. When you get up in the morning, get up in the spirit. Walk in the spirit. Talk in the spirit. Pray in the spirit. Move in the spirit. You are a spiritual being now. You have developed a relationship with God.

No good things come from the flesh. If you want to remain saved, and continue to grow in your relationship with God, you have to be the strongest one in the crowd. You have to be able to be amongst the crowd, and not change. It has to be God. If you want to drink, I am leaving. If you want to listen to the blues, you will have to excuse me. If you decide to hang around, flesh will begin to move and you will start to receive what is going on around you. There is something about the flesh, when it hears something that it likes, it makes your feet begin to move. Some people get more of a kick out of the blues than they do the gospel. You will love one and hate the other. For example: If Betty and I are friends and she loves the blues while I love the gospel, there will be separation between us when it comes to listening to music. It is time for us to make a stand. Stop going along with anything and falling for everything.

We have to learn to see one another in the spirit. It will open your understanding. We have to rejoice in the Lord.

The low state of mind, the defeated spirit, the low self esteem, etc., has to go. You are in God and you are just as great as anyone else. You may not have the gift that I have, but you are still great. If you never preach a sermon, you are still great.

Poor mentality also has to go. God made us to be blessed. Tell poor belief to leave you alone. With God, all things are possible. We have to tell that spirit of sickness that it has to go. God has done everything for us and then he left us a map (the Bible) and a comforter (the Holy Ghost) to lead and guide us. If you are out of the word of God, then you are out of his will. The gloom is gone and now it is time to rejoice.

Isn't it good to know that Jesus loves you in spite of. He is a God that can see the best in us when we are in our worst state. He looks at the good in us when we are cruel and mean. Even when we want to stop and give up, he looks at what we are supposed to be. We belong to him; we are his children. Think about your children: when they were in trouble, and how you went to their rescue. Won't you go and see about your child. Won't you go and give your child a helping hand. That is the same way that God is about us. There is a bond between you and your children, and that is the same bond we need to have with God. I don't care what you have done, God still loves you. I don't care how you act, God still loves you. He loves us and we should take pride in that. We should love him and make the absolute best of everything that he does. When things happen to your child, it hurts you. When people cause your child anguish, it hurts. You can only take but so much. You have to go to your child's aid. That is the same way with God. He will let the devil do only so much to you and he will come to your aid, because you belong to him. He will make a way because you belong to him. He will work a miracle because you belong to him. He will bring you out because you belong to him. God loves us and we belong to him. He can't stand for us to suffer. God is a good God and the best friend we could ever have. Do your very best to develop a loving, trusting, lasting, prosperous, spiritual relationship with God. He is the best thing that could ever happen to us. If that is not reason enough to rejoice, then I don't know what is!!!

My Prayer to God

_____

_____

_____

_____

_____

_____

_____

_____

_____

_____

_____

_____

_____

_____

_____

_____

_____

_____

_____

_____

_____

_____

_____

_____

_____

_____

_____

_____

_____

About the Author

Bishop James E. Clark Sr., and his wife Pastor Linda F. Clark are natives of Bertie County, North Carolina. They are new authors of the book entitled, "Life In The Spirit," which was published, April 21, 2004. They are visionaries of Charity Temple Ministries, with Locations in Aulander, Ahoskie, and Columbia North Carolina.

Bishop Clark received his Bishop accreditation in 1999. He is a renowned preacher, teacher, lecturer, and entrepreneur. Bishop was recognized with the National Leadership Award from the National Congressional Committee in Washington DC, where he served as Business Advisory Council Member.

The Clark's are a ministry on the move. Bishop Clark is a sponsor and donator to community affairs; Charity Temple's Feed the Children Ministry Mobilized Unit, and local food bank distribution. Bishop Clark is a dedicated and contiguous entrepreneur with multiple businesses established (i.e., educational facility, and Charity Temple Transportation Authority.

Bishop and Pastor Clark has a Tape Ministry, Radio Broadcasts, and Gospel, television Commercials.Bishop Clark, and his wife, Linda Clark are prayer partners for God's blessings upon America.

To inquire about tape ordering or for booking, please call (252) 345-0770